Alfred's
PIANO 101

BOOK 1

POPULAR MUSIC FROM MOVIES, TV, RADIO AND STAGE TO PLAY FOR FUN!

CAROL MATZ

Piano 101, Pop Book 1 is designed to be used in conjunction with *Piano 101, Book 1*. The familiar popular pieces were chosen to appeal to teens and adults who are studying piano in group or private lessons. When students reach Unit 4 in *Piano 101, Book 1*, they may begin using this book. Pieces from movies, TV, radio and stage reinforce selected concepts from units 4–15. The popular pieces should be studied simultaneously with the correlating unit and assigned according to the instructions in the upper right corner on the first page of each piece.

The pieces included in the book will be familiar to most students. Due to the melodic range and the harmonic vocabulary of the music, in some cases the pieces that correlate with each unit may be a little more complicated than the music found in the *Piano 101* textbook. To aid with learning, starting positions or keys are identified. Students are asked to identify some notes and intervals in the music. In addition, technical aspects such as moves, stretches, cross-overs and pass-unders are labeled to help students learn the music more quickly. Since the music is familiar, students will be able to play many of the more complex rhythms by ear.

The pieces in *Piano 101, Pop Book 1* are sure to motivate and bring hours of enjoyment to students. Have fun!

Contents

Copyright © MMVIII by ALFRED PUBLISHING CO., INC.
All rights reserved.   Printed in USA.
ISBN-10: 0-7390-5146-6
ISBN-13: 978-0-7390-5146-7

Use with Piano 101, Book 1,
Unit 4, pages 28–38.

This Land Is Your Land

Words and Music by Woody Guthrie
Arranged by Carol Matz

Middle C Position

TEACHER ACCOMPANIMENT (Student plays one octave higher)

3

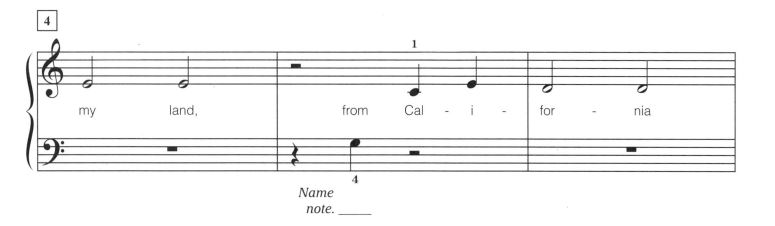

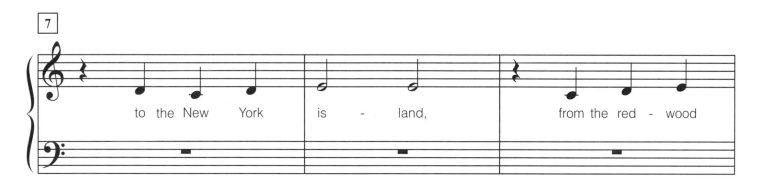

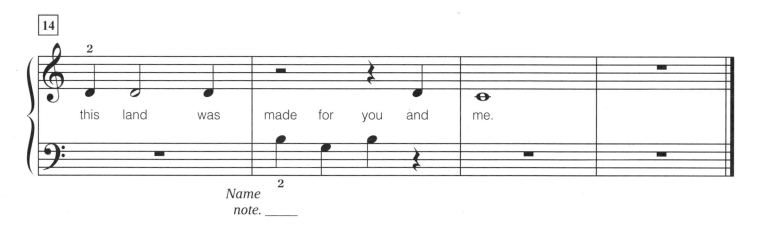

Use with Unit 5, pages 39–49.

Can You Feel the Love Tonight

(from Walt Disney's "The Lion King")

Music by Elton John
Words by Tim Rice
Arranged by Carol Matz

Middle C Position

Name interval. _____

TEACHER ACCOMPANIMENT (Student plays one octave higher)

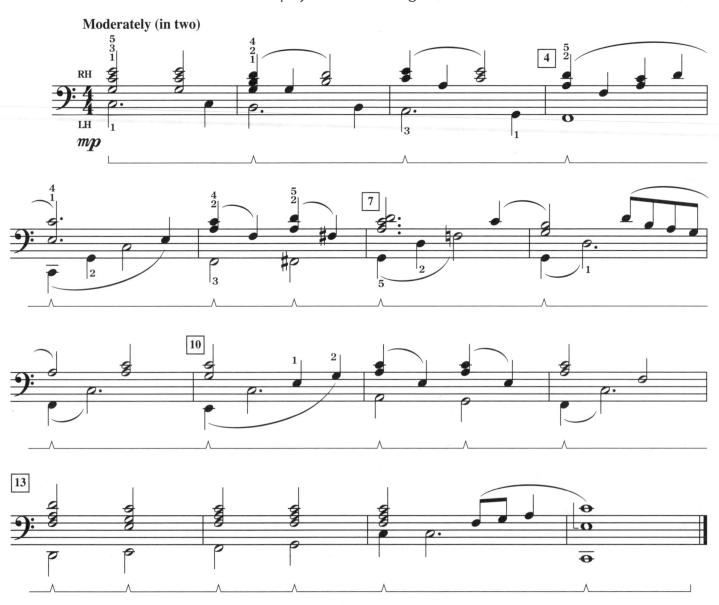

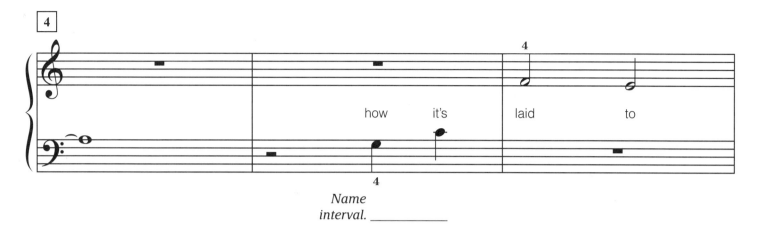

4

how it's laid to

Name
interval. _____

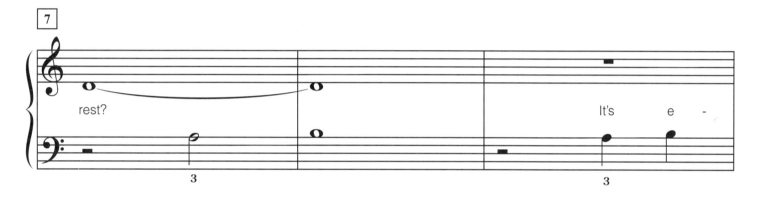

7

rest? It's e -

3   3

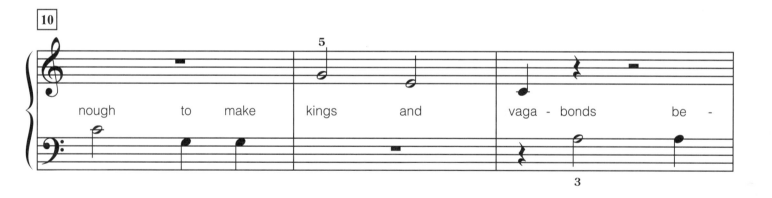

10

nough to make kings and vaga - bonds be -

5   3

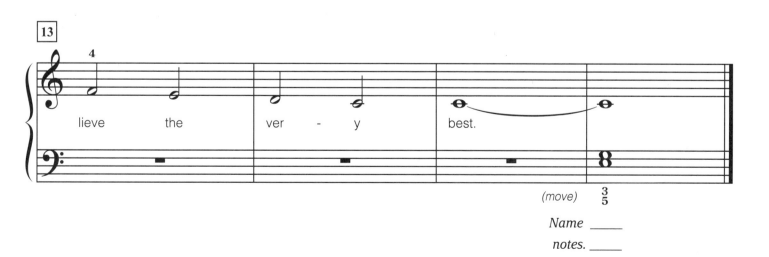

13

lieve the ver - y best.

(move) $\frac{3}{5}$

Name _____
notes. _____

Great Balls of Fire

Words and Music by
Otis Blackwell and Jack Hammer
Arranged by Carol Matz

It's My Party

Words and Music by
Herb Wiener, John Gluck and Wally Gold
Arranged by Carol Matz

RH: Middle C Position
LH: Finger 5 begins on E

8

Use with Unit 7, pages 61–66.

A Whole New World

(from Walt Disney's "Aladdin")

Words by Tim Rice
Music by Alan Menken
Arranged by Carol Matz

Middle C Position

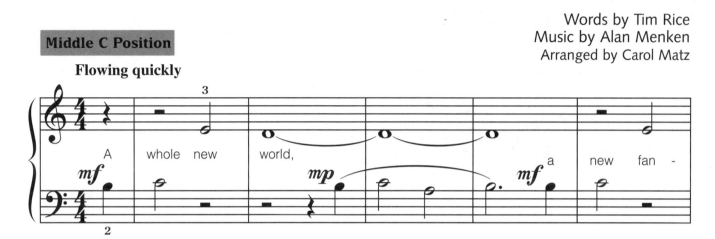

TEACHER ACCOMPANIMENT (Student plays one octave higher)

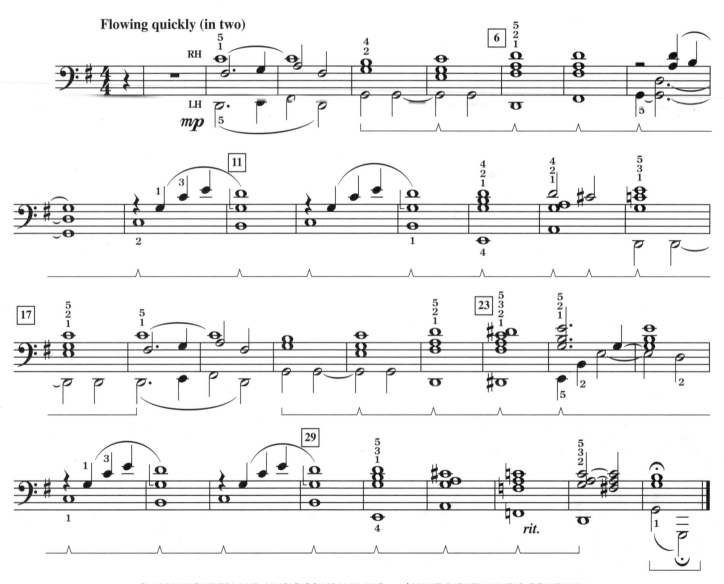

9

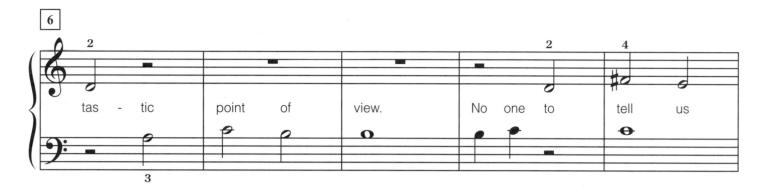

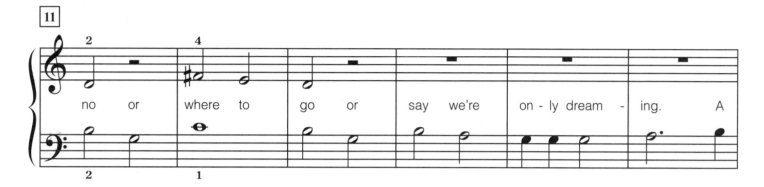

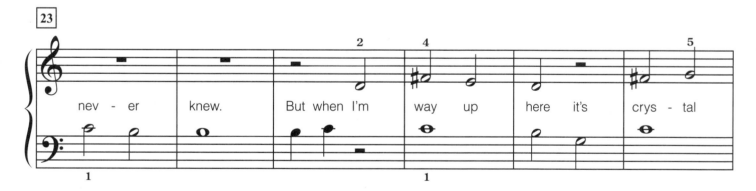

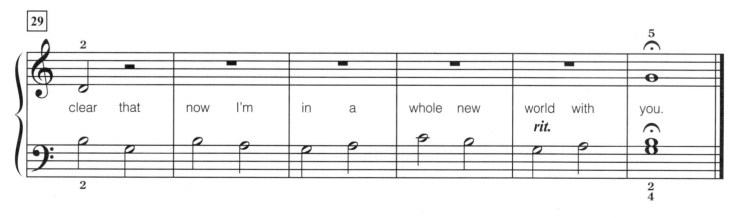

Use with Unit 7, pages 61–66.

James Bond Theme

By Monty Norman
Arranged by Carol Matz

Middle C Position

Quickly; mysteriously

TEACHER ACCOMPANIMENT (Student plays one octave higher)

Quickly; mysteriously

Use with Unit 8, pages 67–76.

Part of Your World

(from Walt Disney's "The Little Mermaid")

Music by Alan Menken
Lyrics by Howard Ashman
Arranged by Carol Matz

Middle C Position

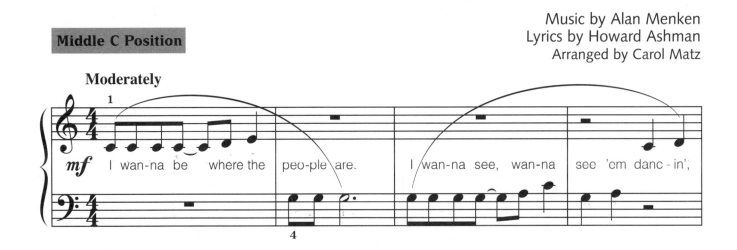

I wan-na be where the peo-ple are. I wan-na see, wan-na see 'em danc-in',

TEACHER ACCOMPANIMENT (Student plays one octave higher)

12

Theme from "New York, New York"

Music by John Kander
Words by Fred Ebb
Arranged by Carol Matz

* Play all eighth notes with an uneven, long-short pattern:

long   short

TEACHER ACCOMPANIMENT (Student plays one octave higher)

Use with Unit 9, pages 77–84.

Ding-Dong! The Witch Is Dead

Key of C Major

Music by Harold Arlen
Lyric by E. Y. Harburg
Arranged by Carol Matz

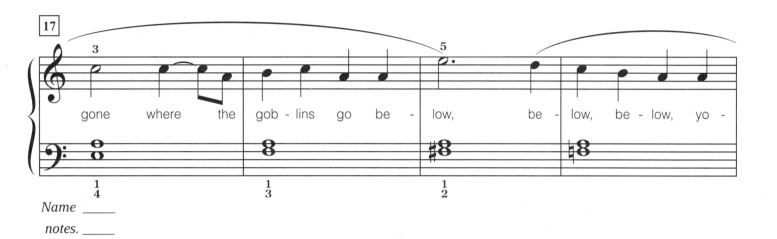

Name ____

notes. ____

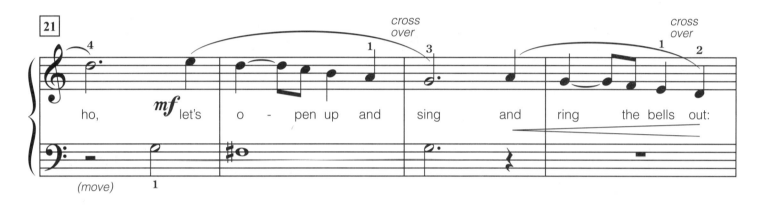

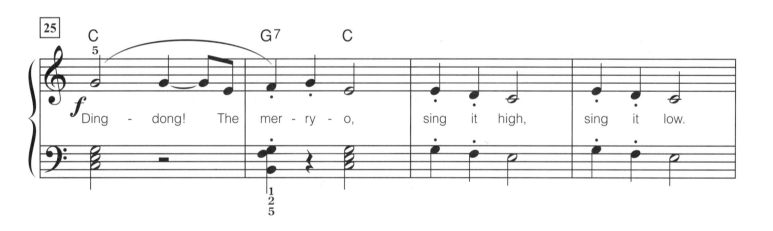

Use with Unit 10, pages 85–94.

Beauty and the Beast

(from Walt Disney's "Beauty and the Beast")

Music by Alan Menken
Lyrics by Howard Ashman
Arranged by Carol Matz

Key of G Major

Smoothly

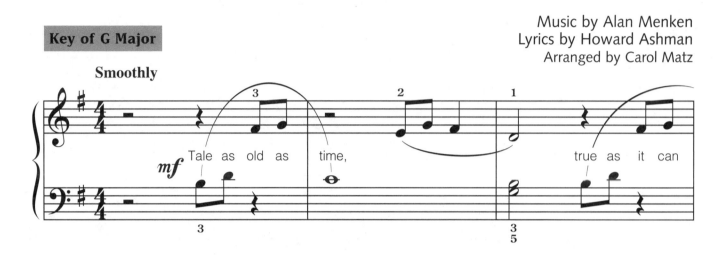

TEACHER ACCOMPANIMENT (Student plays one octave higher)

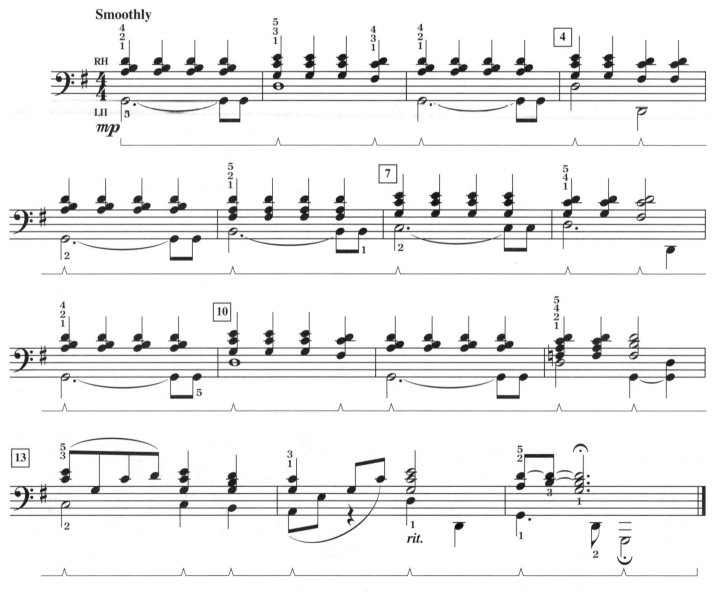

19

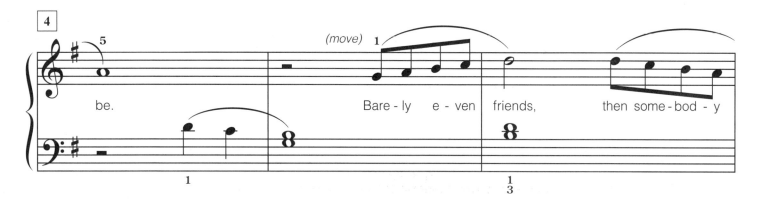

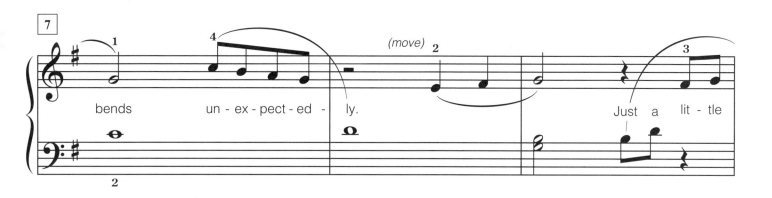

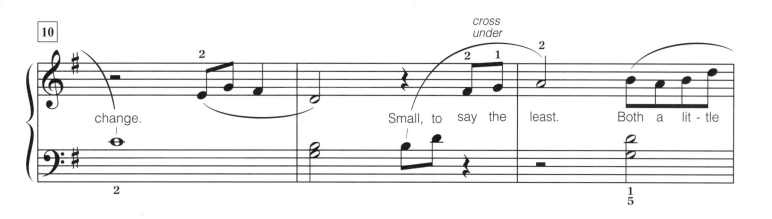

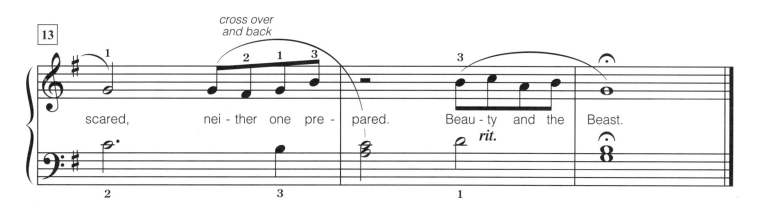

(We're Gonna) Rock Around the Clock

Words and Music by
Max C. Freedman and Jimmy De Knight
Arranged by Carol Matz

Key of G Major

* Play all eighth notes with an uneven, long-short pattern:

long   short

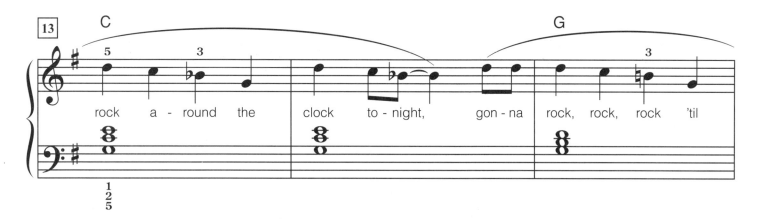

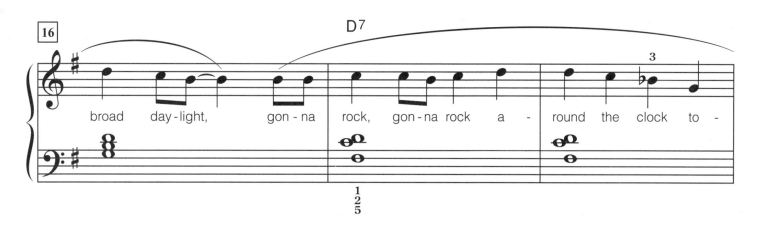

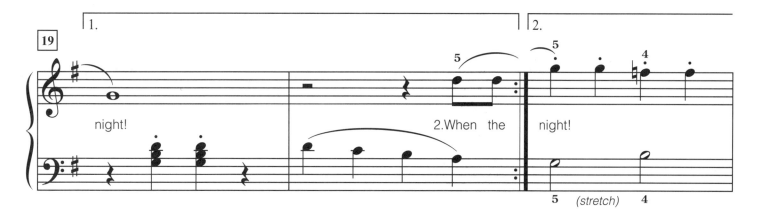

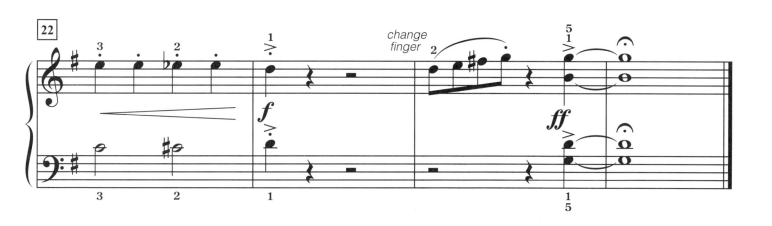

Use with Unit 11, pages 95–100.

Take My Breath Away

Music by Giorgio Moroder
Words by Tom Whitlock
Arranged by Carol Matz

Key of G Major

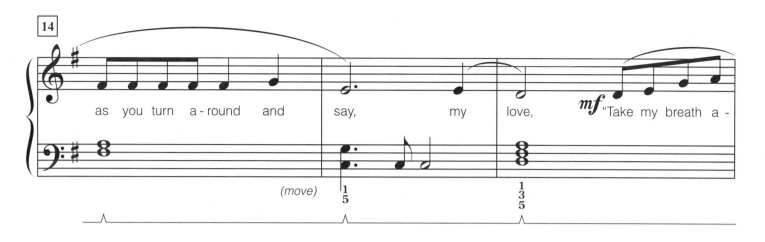

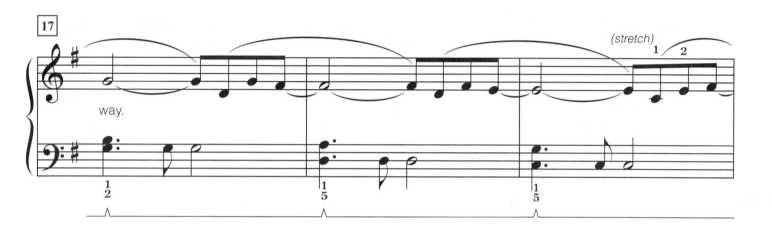

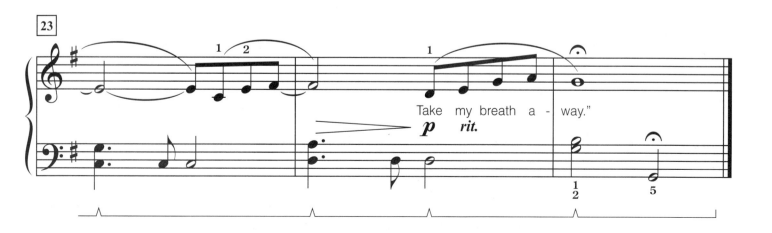

Use with Unit 12, pages 101–109.

What a Wonderful World

Words and Music by
George David Weiss and Bob Thiele
Arranged by Carol Matz

Use with Unit 13, pages 110–118.

Old Time Rock & Roll

Words and Music by
George Jackson and Thomas E. Jones III
Arranged by Carol Matz

Key of G Major

Moderate rock

Use with Unit 14, pages 119–129.

The Lion Sleeps Tonight

Words and Music by
George David Weiss, Hugo Peretti
and Luigi Creatore
Arranged by Carol Matz

Key of F Major

(bring out LH melody)

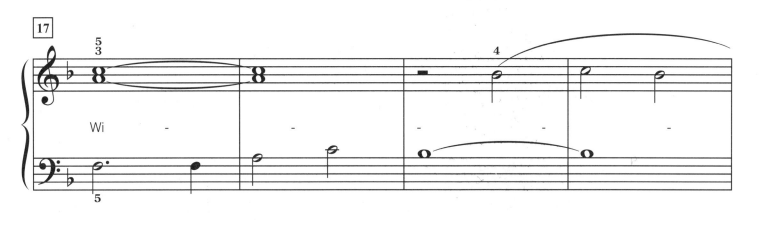

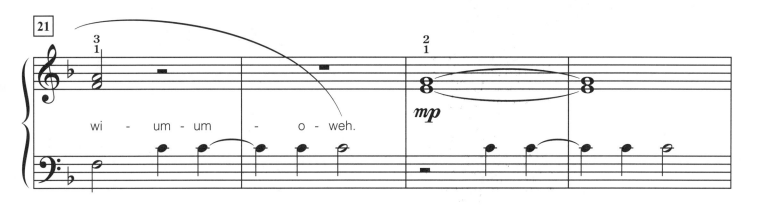

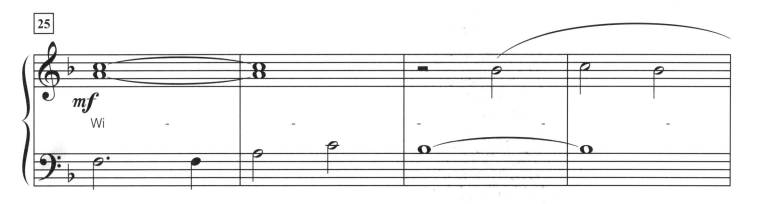

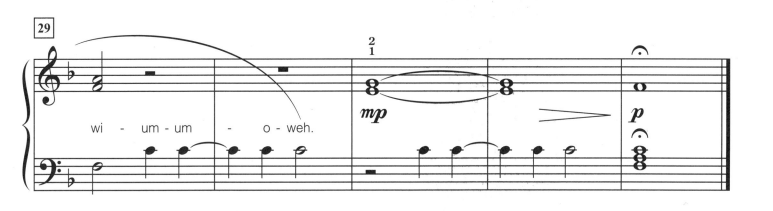

Use with Unit 15, pages 130–137.

> ***D.S. al Coda*** means repeat from the sign 𝄋
> then skip to the Coda (added ending)

Wipe Out

Key of C Major (12-Bar Blues)

By The Surfaris
Arranged by Carol Matz

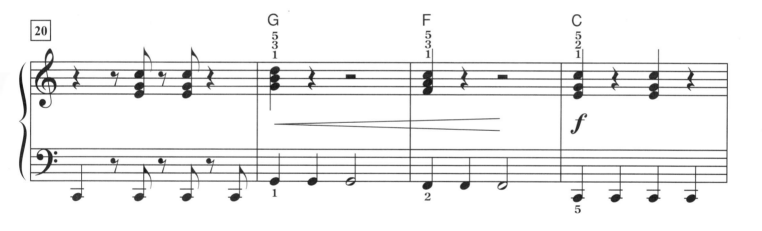

D.S. al Coda

Coda

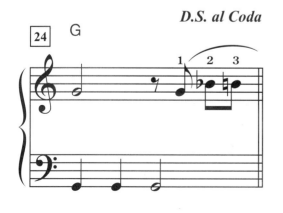

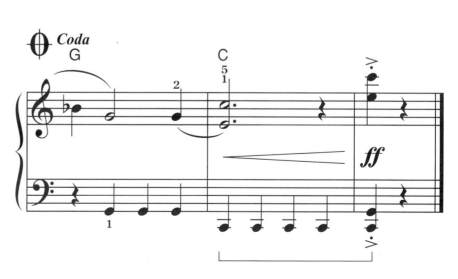